IMAGES OF ENGLAND

Haverhill

Ruffles Mill in 1920. This famous annular windmill was built around 1860 in Wratting Road, and had a circular wind-sail fifty feet in diameter. When it was destroyed during the Second World War, Haverhill lost one of its chief claims to fame, as only four mills of this type were ever erected, and Haverhill's was the last to survive.

IMAGES OF ENGLAND

Haverhill

Roy Brazier
for the Haverhill and District History Group

NONSUCH

An aerial view showing Haverhill in 1936, the town tucked away in a Suffolk valley.

First published 2000
This new pocket edition 2005
Images unchanged from first edition

Nonsuch Publishing Limited
The Mill, Brimscombe Port,
Stroud, Gloucestershire, GL5 2QG
www.nonsuch-publishing.com

British Library Cataloguing in Publication Data.
A catalogue record for this book is available from the British Library.

ISBN 1-84588-150-8

Typesetting and origination by Nonsuch Publishing Limited
Printed in Great Britain by Oaklands Book Services Limited

Contents

A map of Haverhill, 1925.

Introduction

The market town of Haverhill stands in the south-west corner of Suffolk, close to the junction of the boundaries of Essex and Cambridgeshire, and is on a tributary of the Suffolk River Stour. Like many other ancient towns of England, the origins of Haverhill are lost in the mists of antiquity. The earliest mention of it is in the Domesday Book, compiled in 1086 by the order of William the Conqueror, but it must have been an inhabited place at least 1,000 years before this as in 1788 an urn containing about fifty gold Roman coins was dug up near Place Farm. This was one of the most remarkable archaeological discoveries to be made in the district, but unfortunately we know little about it, as many of the coins disappeared shortly after the find.

The town was probably first settled permanently around the beginning of the eleventh century, and the place name 'Haver' meaning 'barley', indicates that it was in a grain growing district. The Domesday Book tells us that there was a market and it is to this that Haverhill owes its early importance. Haverhill does not figure much in subsequent chronicles, and during the Middle Ages it passed a peaceful and quiet existence, only occasionally being noted in public records. A castle is referred to several times in the thirteenth and fourteenth centuries, but it was never more than a fortified Manor House on high ground to the north west of the town, and nothing remains today.

Until the fourteenth century the town was essentially an agricultural quarter enjoying the privileges of a weekly market and two annual fairs, on 12 May and 10 October. The latter one was finally abolished in 1872, the market day being held on a Friday. During the Middle Ages, Haverhill became one of the lesser wool towns of East Anglia, and the weaving tradition, then established, became a very important factor in its future prosperity. In the seventeenth century the refugee Huguenot and Flemish weavers, fleeing from religious persecution in their own countries, found a haven in eastern England. A number of these new immigrants found their way to Haverhill, bringing with them their methods of weaving which they practised and also taught to the town's inhabitants. There are records of cloth from Haverhill being sold in

London in the seventeenth century. The wool trade eventually died out and was replaced by the manufacture of checks and fustians, a trade which subsisted until around 1800. Silks and drabbets then came to the fore and a number of silk factories were built. All this was changed in 1856 when the firm of D. Gurteen and Son, which had been first established some sixty or seventy years before, became the principal undertaking by introducing the steam loom, a position it maintained for many years.

A disaster befell Haverhill in 1667 when a great fire destroyed a large part of the town, leaving, it was stated, just one house and a pear tree. This is the main reason why there are not many ancient buildings standing today; those that remain were not in the path of the seventeenth-century flames. Other fires occurred in 1775 and 1776 to further reduce some of the more picturesque dwellings, while a severe plague in 1768 caused seventy-nine deaths in one year.

A great change came over the town within the space of the last 150 years, and from being a quiet and sleepy place, considered by its neighbours to be decidedly a backwater, it became a busy manufacturing centre. First came the Victorian period when many fine buildings, civic and otherwise, were built in the town, the schools in 1877, the town hall in 1883 and the Old Independent Church in 1884. Haverhill is also looked upon as the nonconformist capital of the region with many different places of worship throughout the town.

The two world wars in the first half of the twentieth century, plus a progressive town council, combined to hasten the advance of Haverhill. The population had been mounting slowly: in 1801 it stood at 1,104, in 1841 it had nearly doubled to 2,159 and by 1911 it had risen further to 4,749. The first council houses were built in Haverhill in the 1920s with electricity coming along in 1930. Between the end of the Second World War and 1949, sixty-eight new dwellings were built by the Haverhill Urban District Council, and the Parkway estate to the west of the town was quickly coming into being. Towards the end of the 1950s an expansion scheme was initiated between the Haverhill UDC and the London County Council, which swelled the population considerably and brought with it numerous other industries from the capital, together with their workers who moved into the new houses provided. This face-lift changed Haverhill beyond belief, and it is continuing to grow steadily day by day to become one of the largest towns in East Anglia. Large estates now surround the town to replace the commons of the early years, including the Clements, Chalkstone and Chimswell. As well as being twinned with towns in France and Germany, Haverhill enjoys a happy relationship with Haverhill, Massachusetts, in the United States of America, which was founded in 1641 by members of the Ward family from Haverhill in Suffolk.

Roy Brazier
August 1999

Acknowledgements

Thanks to all the members of the Local History Group for all the help they have given me in putting this publication together.

One

Town Centre

An early photograph of the parish church of St Mary's, situated in the centre of the town. The small chapel adjoining the east wall has since been demolished. On the left is the old Corn Exchange built in 1857, which later became the office of the town's newspaper, the *South West Suffolk Echo*.

From the tower of St Mary's in 1900 can be seen the many alleyways and yards leading off Queen Street, which runs from the junction with Swan Lane (mid-right) to the top left corner. In the foreground is the cluster of ancient cottages occupying Peas Hill, which were all removed, leaving an open space which has become the town's new Market Square. Top right is the railway station and goods yard, with Taylor's Corn Mill, built in 1860, and the police station and courthouse, built in 1886, in front of it.

Opposite above: The town centre as seen in 1868. The house on the left occupied most of the west churchyard, and has long gone. Buildings from the right are: a small shop, the early home of the Gurteen family, the Bell Hotel, with a ladder against its front, a small chemist shop, and a cottage garden (see opposite below).

Opposite below: An 1880 photograph shows the small cottage and garden which survived until the Co-operative Society headquarters was built in 1896. The left hand shop belonged to Mr Lee, a measure maker, while Mr Wooding, a saddler, lived next door in the cottage. The Argus store now stands on this site.

Seen from Mill Road in 1880 are some of the cottages which stood on Peas Hill, the oldest part of the town. These were the last of the old town centre buildings to be demolished. The shop on the left is now a chemists shop.

Miss Esther Sparrow's corner sweet shop with children surrounding its windows in 1900. Fined in 1883 for opening on a Sunday, it occupied the corner of the High Street and Swan Lane, now Peacock's shop.

Right: A view east of the church in 1889. The small brick-built shop on the left, which survived until the late 1960s, was a shoemakers. The building on the right was replaced in the 1930s and became the butcher's department of the Co-op, then Murrays, and is now the 'Drabbet Smock', a public house .

Below: St Mary's Church in 1911. Destroyed by the 1667 fire, which started nearby in the orchard of the Swan Inn in Swan Lane, the church was rebuilt by 1670. The ornamental gateway and iron railings around the churchyard were taken down during the Second World War for the war effort. The main door gates were spared as they were part of Edward VII's Coronation celebrations. Note that the small chapel on the side of the church has now gone.

For many years the vicar and his choir have climbed St Mary's tower on Ascension Day to hold a special service. This photograph was taken in 1950 and some older members of the congregation have joined the young choir boys.

The interior of the parish church, a quiet oasis in the busy town centre. Part of the rear of the church is now divided by folding doors to provide a social area. The doors are still opened up for special occasions. One monument in the church is to John Ward who helped settle Haverhill, Massachusetts in New England.

Right: This was the first home of the Co-op in 1882. The cottage in Peas Hill was hired by the company. Mr S. Webb was the part time storekeeper on four evenings a week, and all day on Friday and Saturday. The first day's takings were £19 2s 7½d.

Below: The Co-operative Society's second home stood east of the church, next to the tower, *c.* 1900. The staff of the shop stand proudly outside their premises, including two butcher's assistants and a delivery cart.

Market Hill, Haverhill. 4

Left: It is Market Day in 1948 and the stalls stretched quite a distance up the High Street. Most of the traders at that time had only small vehicles, and as these did not take up too much space, they would park them at the rear of their stalls.

Below: When floods hit the town in 1958, the town centre was awash for a while. The Co-op shop staff with other helpers are trying valiantly to stem the tide of the rising water, which happened quite suddenly between the hours of six and nine in the morning.

Part of the large crowd which gathered to see the opening of the new Co-operative Stores in 1896, with most of the people wanting to get into the picture. Two shops and a house had been demolished to make way for the new premises. The opening ceremony was performed by Mr Ben Jones, the manager of the London Branch. An exhibition, showing the type of goods the customers could expect, biscuits, jams, shoes, clothing, sweets and soaps, was also opened by Lord John Henry on the same day. Other departments later added were the gents' outfitters, ladies' department, and a dairy. In 1904 some stables were built, and then farms were purchased at Shudy Camps in 1911 and Hazelstubb Farm, Haverhill, in 1918. Another branch was opened in Clare in 1929.

Above: This house in the High Street, pictured in 1893, was converted into the front office for D. Gurteen and Sons factory. It was previously the residence of D. Gurteen (1777–1856), birthplace of another D. Gurteen (1809) and of D. Gurteen Jnr (1834). Left to right: Rowlingson (boy), Bridge, Mann, Bullock, Deeks, Backler. The Haverhill post office moved to this site in 1933.

Left: The building seen here in 1900, was operating as the Anchor Coffee Tavern for some years at the end of the nineteenth century, and it had closed by the time this photograph was taken. The enterprise attempted to curb the evils of the demon beer-drinking in the town.

Looking down the High Street in 1895 towards the church. The original Corn Exchange is on the left, the upper part of it being used as a furniture warehouse. When its foundations were being dug up, two small brick ovens were found, these being left in their places. The building also housed the local courtroom for a time and a reading room. The area in front of the old Corn Exchange was the site of the original market place, and nearby stood the stocks and the pillory, last used in 1815, and the market cross, removed in 1829. The Corn Market outgrew its building, which was bought by the Temperance Society in 1887, and a larger Corn Exchange opened in Withersfield Road in 1889.

The High Street in 1884 showing in more detail the Anchor Coffee Tavern, set up by the Temperance Movement. The house on the right is Chauntry House, later to become part of the Playhouse cinema. The top half can still be seen today, above Watsons and the Ipswich Building Society.

Gurteen's Factory gates shown here in 1937 decorated for the Coronation of George VI. Lloyds Bank on the left was built on the site of the old Greyhound Coaching Inn. A small concrete greyhound's head can still be seen on the wall just inside the factory gates.

Under nine

George III

Nobody knows when we started business in Haverhill; certainly not later than 1784, maybe much earlier.

Our first activity was weaving and this continues today, but quite early in our career we started to make Smocks, many of which were very elaborate, a typical one being the "Waggoner" which is illustrated on this page.

1784

D. GURTEEN & SONS LTD.
Chauntry Mills, Haverhill, Suffolk

Right: An advertisement for D. Gurteen and Sons factory from 1954, shows the type of smocks that used to be made for the farm workers, each with its own pattern depicting their trade. This one portrays a waggoner.

Below: Part of the main sewing machine room in Gurteen's factory in 1900, showing how large the workstaff was at the time. Most of the townsfolk about this time worked in some way for the Gurteen family.

Right: Three generations of the notable Gurteen family of Haverhill seen in 1892. This shows Daniel Gurteen Snr (1809–1893), seated, his son, standing on the left, Daniel Gurteen Jnr (1834–1894), and his grandson, standing on the right, Daniel Maynard Gurteen (1872–1952).

Below: Chapman's shop, seen here in 1960, was originally the Market Hill Chapel, built in 1839. Chapmans moved into the old building in the early 1930s. For many years the old penny farthing bicycle stood on the top of the shop, and although now taken down, remains stored in the town.

Two

High Street to the Hamlet

A bird's eye view of the beginning of the High Street with the Coffee Tavern again prominent, lower left in 1878. Other buildings left to right are: T. Wright (wine merchant), Bates & Son (grocers and drapers), F.W. Bates (a private house), J. Arbour (builder), Munford & Co (fancy repostory), E.W. Griggs (chemist), W. Newman (ironmonger), Pannell Brothers (brewers) later the White Horse, and the London County Bank.

A view which is nearly identical to the previous page but dated from much later, in 1950. Top left can be seen the 'Meadows' a favourite walk for many years, but now part of the relief road. The footpath to Kedington passed under the railway bridge in the top left corner. The coach is just leaving the town centre bus stop, which was used until the new coach station was opened on the Relief Road. Many of the houses and shops in the High Street had extensive gardens to the rear. In place of the Coffee Tavern is now Boots the Chemist, Bates is now Head's shop while L. Simmons is on the site of Munfords. At No. 27 Atterton & Ellis has taken over the ironmonger's shop of Newmans which had also belonged to William Poole for a considerable time. The London County Bank has now become the Westminster Bank. Note the missing chimney of the old Corn Exchange in the foreground.

Opposite above: Chauntry House, one of the finest buildings in the town. When the Playhouse Cinema was built, the entrance was through the front door; later a larger entrance was made in place of the left hand window. The main cinema was built in the garden (see opposite below).

Opposite below: The garden of Chauntry House before the cinema was erected. Daniel Gurteen is sitting reading at one set of French doors, and his wife Caroline at another.

A view almost from the same spot as on the previous page, but some years later, around 1880, showing the newly reconstructed Chauntry House. The roof has undergone a transformation to make the building appear grander than it was previously. Some sort of pavement has also been made in the form of cobblestones. On the extreme left is the post office while the horse and cart stands outside the White Horse beerhouse. Note the two small faces looking from the top window of Chauntry House.

Opposite above: Atterton and Ellis's retail shop in 1960. Since they were renowned for their lawn mower grinding machines, mowers take pride of place outside the shop. The small windows each side of the door are full with lines of Dinky toy models.

Opposite below: An earlier view of the High Street, c. 1868. The original Chauntry House is shown on the right, while nearby is the knife and scissors grinder working away on his specially adapted bicycle. Note the roadway is still quite unkept, and the pedestrians have no real pavement.

A Sunday School procession winds its way down the High Street, most of the children wearing their neat little boaters and bonnets. This turn of the century scene shows on the right the front of the Greyhound Inn and some men standing near the railings of the Market Hill Chapel.

Another Sunday School procession at the turn of the century, this time going in the opposite direction. The school teacher is gently herding her young children at the head of the banner. These occasions joined together groups of several denominations.

Looking west to the Market Place in 1934. The Playhouse cinema is shown clearly on the left while on the right is the familiar sign of the 'Golden Boot' over Charles Baker's shop.

The Empire Cinema was opened in 1912 being built on to the rear of 39 High Street, the home of Dr Goodman. Haverhill's first cinema was the Premier Picture Palace in the back garden of a house in Chauntry Road in 1911. (Drawing by Elizabeth Lines)

An 1890 photograph with most of the post office staff posing outside their High Street premises, together with two of the post office traps which delivered and collected the mail from other nearby towns. Munford's Fancy Bazaar stands next to the tall brick building, Hoveton House. Mr E. Griggs the chemist, pictured second right, was the local chemist who also ran the post office. All the buildings in this photograph have been demolished, and modern shops now occupy this site.

Opposite above: The scene, in 1883, after fire destroyed Mr Taylor's house in the High Street. On the left is Helions House, another of the large houses which adorned Haverhill in the past. The burned out site was bought by Mr D. Gurteen and added to his residence next door. Note the old milestone in the right hand wall.

Opposite below: A 1960s view of the building which replaced Mr Taylor's ruins. Cleales was not the first garage on this spot; they took over Mr Turpin's Central Garage. Note how the petrol pump lines had to be stretched across the pavement to reach the cars.

Helions House, as seen in 1960, one of the pillared porch houses formerly in the High Street. Its large and very fine gardens at the rear were often the venue for garden fêtes. Once a doctor's surgery, it is now the site of Woolworths.

Across the road from Woolworths is Barclays Bank. The entrance to the Empire Cinema was down the passageway between the bank and Wilkins' shop. The bank was formerly the home of Dr Goodman; it also served as the Home Guard headquarters during the last war. Note the special offers at the International Stores on the left.

Wilkins and Co., the men's and boys' outfitters, pictured in 1925. They were established in Haverhill in the nineteenth century, taking over Mr Hunt's shop at 41 High Street. They were one of the first businesses to have their own delivery van.

Although forty years have passed, the appearance of Wilkins' shop has not really altered a great deal, as this 1960s photograph shows. The shop is now Dolland & Aitchison's.

Above: In the 1950s the High Street still has the charm of a small market town. The shops lining the street are mainly family businesses. Within the next decade this view was to change dramatically.

Right: George Carter stands proudly in the doorway of his small but select jewellery shop in 1916. It is still a jewellery shop but the sign above the door now reads Griffith Jones.

The date is 1920 and Mr W. Hammond is all ready to go out on his delivery round with Thomas Jarvis's trade bicycle.

A busy High Street scene consisting mainly of children, some of whom cannot stand still for the camera, c. 1900. Outside the Red Lion on the right, two ladies seem to be supporting themselves to stay steady.

Farrant's greengrocery shop, here seen in 1959, was one of the best known shops in the town for numerous years. Mr Farrant lived at Sturmer, a nearby village, and during his younger days was a fine footballer and later a referee.

Opposite above: Claydon's shop and garage, seen here in 1910, was established at 49 High Street in 1895. It had a workshop dealing with cycle repairs and sales, together with the sole agency for Singer Sewing machines. Mr Claydon expanded into the new motor car trade later and installed a petrol pump on the forecourt.

Opposite below: Edward Jennings took over the business as this 1960 photograph shows. He moved in during the 1930s. Radio and television was then the main business, with a van delivering around the villages with wireless accumulators and HT batteries.

The imposing front of the Haverhill town hall has remained little changed over the years. Costing £5,000, this building was built and presented to the town in 1883 by Daniel Gurteen senior, to celebrate his golden wedding. When new, it housed the public library, council chamber and a large concert hall. Electricity was installed in 1948. It has recently re-opened after a massive interior renovation, and includes a cinema, café, and the history centre.

Above: One of the dance bands in Haverhill between the two world wars was led by Tommy Turner who played many times for the dances in the Town Hall. Members here, around 1934, are left to right: Percy Page, A. Chapman, Tommy Turner, Muriel Turner and Mr Linsell.

Below: This fine organ was installed in the town hall as a gift from D. Gurteen Jnr, and cost £1,000. Its height is shown by the relief caretaker David Dunn standing alongside, *c.* 1980. It has since been removed, and is now stored at the Cotton Musical Museum near Stowmarket.

Members of Haverhill Urban District Council in 1900, lined up outside the town hall. Left to right, back row: C. Boardman, J. Beasley, R. Ruffle, A.J. Simpson. Middle row: J. Gurteen, E.M. Green, T. Jarvis, F.D. Unwin, H.D. Taylor. Front row (standing): C. French, J.J. Knewstubbs (surveyor), S.H. Graham (clerk), F. Perry. Seated: W.B. Gurteen (chairman).

Opposite above: A crowded dance floor in 1948 for a popular Saturday night dance in the town hall. During the Second World War the attendance was swelled by the fact that four RAF bases surrounded the town, together with other units of the armed forces. Those who were unable to gain admission could go into the balcony and watch for a small fee.

Opposite below: Senior citizens were not forgotten and numerous Christmas parties were held in the concert room, this one in 1960. The famous balcony can be seen at the back, while on the walls each side of the doorway are a shield bearing the names of those Haverhill forces mentioned in dispatches in the Second World War. To the right is a plaque given to the town by their namesake in the USA.

The very ornate shop front of Thomas Jarvis's High Street premises, c. 1880. He was a grocer, draper and tea dealer who started as an apprentice with Mr Hunt. He took over the business when Mr Hunt passed away.

A view taken from just outside the town hall in 1890, with people, prams and horse-drawn vehicles. On the right is the entrance to the yard and workshops of Mason and Son, builders, and next door the black gates of Green the stonemason. The tall brick building is Cambridge House.

A serene moment looking west down the High Street, with the new town hall peeping over the buildings on the left, c. 1885. The small children, left, are sitting on the step of 52 High Street, which eventually became a shop for a succession of photographers in the town, ending with C.W. Davey.

Eden Place pictured in 1975, just before being demolished. This was a hidden quarter on the High Street/Eden Road corner reached by a dim passage.

A small part of the High Street which has more or less survived the march of progress, as seen, c. 1962. The passage to Eden Place can be seen between Jim's Tackle shop and Patricia Georgina's, now a taxi office. Chinese and Indian takeaways are now on this spot.

Many street parties were held in Haverhill to celebrate the end of the Second World War. This one was in Eden Road

The old White Hart public house at the top of the High Street in 1960, on the corner of Duddery Hill, a very dangerous part of the High Street which was extremely narrow at this spot. The pub has now been demolished and rebuilt further back, thus improving this corner considerably.

Just around the corner from the busy High Street stood this old row of cottages, in Duddery Lane (now Hill) pictured around 1880. Note the unmade surface of the road.

The Mount was one of the largest houses of Victorian Haverhill. In the second half of the nineteenth century it was the home of Mr William Wakeling Boreham. He was a brewer and astronomer and a member of the Royal Astronomical Society. It is probable that he had some sort of observatory here. Later it became the home of Daniel Maynard Gurteen. This photograph was taken before 1884, as the present Old Independent Church had not been built. After a spell as a hostel for factory workers from Addis Brush Works in Colne Valley Road, it was demolished in the mid-1960s.

Opposite above: A group of young ladies calling themselves the 'Young Helpers League', pictured in the gardens of the Mount during the summer of 1908.

Opposite below: A pleasant scene in the gardens of the Mount, before the days of the vacuum cleaner. The four gentlemen are busy beating a large carpet which is spread out on the tennis court. They are William Webb, Freddie Ford, Bill Reade and Freddie's father.

The interior of the Mount, showing the old ornate staircase, which was reputed to have come from nearby Horseheath Hall when it was pulled down in the eighteenth century.

The modern look-a-like houses which have been built on the site of the Mount.

Above: Duddery Terrace, an unaltered part of the High Street, was built by D. Gurteen in 1878, on part of the gardens of the Mount which stood opposite. The corner shop has been a butcher's for most of its life, Norman Pryke taking it over from J.W. Sawyer.

Below: The spire of the Old Independent Church dominates this 1890 view looking down Hamlet Road, with the Weavers' Arms sign on the right. The borders of Essex and Suffolk crossed the road at this time.

Above: One of the many blacksmith's shops in the town, *c.* 1880. This one stood in Hamlet Road, on the spot now occupied by the small neat lawn and garden beside the Old Independent Church.

Left: The Old Independent Church with its lofty spire, a town landmark for many years. The church was founded in 1662 by Stephen Scandaret, and after holding their meetings in private houses, the congregation erected a Meeting House in 1715. The present building dates from 1885.

Right: Mr Percy Kibble, a well-known figure in the town for many years. As well as being the organist for the Old Independent Church he taught music at Haverhill Schools.

Below: The Weavers, one of the very few medieval houses that have survived in Haverhill, *c.* 1880. The open hall is the boarded section to the left. The building was also one of the first schools in the town. Miss Grace Gurteen, the Local History Group's President for many years, lived here. It now houses offices and at the time of this photograph it was the photographic establishment of Charles Vizon.

The Weavers, in 1870, showing the cross wing when it was jettied. Note the large gates on the right, now Colne Valley Road. This road split the gardens of the Mount into two portions.

Cleves House in Hamlet Road as it was in 1912. Thought to have been built in the sixteenth century as part of the marriage settlement to Ann of Cleves from Henry VIII, although she never lived here. It was anciently the manor house of the Beaumont family, who added the curious arched veranda after the Napoleonic Wars, and also for many years the vicarage for St Mary's.

In 1974, Cleves House was restored and the façade removed. The grouped diagonal and octagonal brick chimneys remain as one of its most striking features, and on the stack at the south end is a sun dial. After some years as a private nursing home, it is now the offices of a company which appreciates its history.

The Hamlet Croft in Hamlet Road was for a great many years the home of outdoor events in Haverhill, including the traditional August Bank Holiday Gala, established in 1887. It is also the home of Haverhill Rovers Football Club. This frail looking grandstand was a temporary structure for the 1902 Coronation celebrations, but later a more substantial stand was put up for spectators.

Before Haverhill Rovers became the top football team, Haverhill Town were the ones to follow. They were formed around 1880 and played in light blue and dark blue halves. When the Rovers formed around 1888, the Town found it hard going and they amalgamated with the Rovers towards the end of the nineteenth century. This photograph, believed to be the only one of Haverhill Town, was taken in 1891, when they reached the final of the Suffolk Junior Cup before losing narrowly to Halesworth at Portman Road, Ipswich. One of their matches was at Felixstowe, whither they had to travel by train, and after arriving at the railway station they then had to walk over two miles to the Felixstowe football ground. They still won through however. The team members were: A. Backler (goal), J. Backler and G. Burton (backs), E. Backler, D. Gowers and F. Shipp (halves), L. Backler, W. Tilbrook, H. Noble, C. Jobson and W. Radford (forwards). Radford with 2 and Jobson with 1 were the Town's goalscorers.

Haverhill Rovers pictured at the end of the 1946/47 season which was one of their best ever, winning six cups and being runners-up in two more. This season they put out three teams each week.

Hamlet Road seen in 1932. The handsome looking house called 'Elmhurst' is on the right, and was, for some years, the residence of the Smart family. Further on the right is the Private School of the Misses Ashplant. Note on the left the street light and the traffic sign denoting a 10mph speed limit.

September 1904 saw one of the biggest fires in the town at the premises of Atterton & Ellis on Hamlet Green. It started in the saw-pit in the late evening and caused £2,000 worth of damage. John Atterton started his business in 1874 in Duddery Road and moved to the old Silk Factory on Hamlet Green in 1883.

Vale Place is another of Haverhill's older buildings which have somehow survived. Built in the late eighteenth century, it has been vacant for a long period and is now looking decidedly run down. An open-air swimming pool was constructed in the grounds in 1907, and behind the house was the Heasworth Brick Co.

A 1980 bird's eye view of the Haverhill Hamlet area of the town. Running across the bottom is the tree-lined track bed of Haverhill's disused railway, while the new sewerage works is bottom right. New factories line the relief road on the right, and top left is the Holland's Road industrial estate. Mid left shows Vale Place surrounded by the new housing of Beaumont Court and Beaumont Vale, and beyond them the wide open space of the Hamlet Croft, once a notorious slope on the football ground which has since been levelled.

The country lane, featured here around 1880, leads off Hamlet Green to the villages of Helions and Steeple Bumpstead, and is naturally called Bumpstead Road. This view is virtually unrecognizable now as it has been widened and takes much more traffic.

A Haverhill landmark for all those who approach the town from the east, seen here around 1900. This railway viaduct was built in 1865 to link the two different railways which served Haverhill, the Colne Valley and the Great Eastern Company.

Three

Queen Street
to Withersfield Road

The junction of Swan Lane/Camps Road and High Street/Queen Street (looking down Queen Street) as seen in 1910. The building with the 'Peas Hill Slade' sign is Jarvis the butcher's and could have been one of the houses that was reputed to have been taken down at Hundon and re-erected here after the great fire in 1667. Note the sign of a lost Haverhill pub, the Star, in Queen Street.

Heavy snowfalls in 1959 nearly brought the town to a halt, but improvising with a tractor and trailer, the milk was delivered. This scene is outside Backler's shop near the Queen Street and Swan Lane corner.

The old Workhouse buildings were swamped in 1958, and the flood water ran through the disused building and out through the back windows into the Pightle river.

Queen Street was previously flooded in 1903, when this picture was taken.

A rather drier picture of the shoe shop of Archie Backler in Queen Street in the 1960s. Note his 'bargain window' and the booking facility for a production by the Haverhill Dramatic Players.

Queen Street looking west in 1911. The group on the left are outside the post office which later became Graham's the chemist. The tall building in the distance is the Temperance Hotel, now the site of the Council Offices.

One of the best known shops in Queen Street in recent years was R.C. Poole, confectioner, stationer and tobacconist, seen here in 1968.

Right: Behind the shops in Queen Street was the Infirmary, built in 1840, costing £2,200. It took in the lame and sick poor from the Workhouse on the opposite side of the street. It is seen here in its ruined state around 1965.

Below: On the site of the Workhouse and the rambling Union Square has risen this new small shopping precinct, given the name of Queens Square.

A. Clarke's, one of the small family shops which lined Queen Street in bygone days. The shop's wares are prominently displayed in the window.

Queens Street from the west, c. 1900. The buildings on the left have all disappeared now, but on the right many remain, including Ellis's Bakery, still going strong. The railings in the right belong to the Temperance Hotel.

The yard of G.&J. Hayward carriage builders in 1879. This scene shows, on the left, the raw materials (logs) and on the right the finished work (three finely made carriages).

The classic AA patrolman's motor cycle combination stands in the front of Hayward's Garage in 1958. Cars took over from the Carriage Works by 1920. This garage was both AA and RAC recommended and was the parcels agent for the Eastern Counties Bus Company.

Before the Woolpack Inn occupied the corner of Queen Street and Wratting Road, this house stood on the spot, the cottage of a Mr Basham, whose daughter Caroline married Daniel Gurteen.

Opposite the Woolpack stand the Haverhill Board Schools opened in 1877. This is how they looked in 1880 before the clock was added in the tower. This is now known as the Cangle Junction and has been converted into special housing by English Church Housing.

In 1920 the girls were taught PE in the rear playground, accompanied here by their teacher at the upright piano. The corrugated building on the left is the woodwork room.

The Boys Council School football team, winners of the West Suffolk Schools Cup in 1934. Left to right, back row: Mr A. Smith, S. Pavey, D. Freeman, Mr D.M. Gurteen, H. Archer, P. Pavey, Mr P.W. Underwood (headmaster). Middle row: L. Peck, A. Aves, G. Nunn, R. Mansfield, C. Farrant. Front row: C. Peverett, J. Poole, J. Keeble.

Left: The two champions at the Council School Sports in 1930, Horace Willis and Beatrice Archer.

Below: The Cangle School changed names frequently and this is the first year as the Haverhill Secondary School in 1920. They used the West End church schoolroom for a while before moving back across the road to the main school buildings.

The Rose and Crown Inn looks slightly ragged in this photograph of 1883. The man with the handcart may just have brought someone's luggage from the Great Eastern Railway station not many yards away.

Looking from Station Road across the junction, and showing the Rose and Crown Inn with its first extension in 1893. J. Henderson's shop later became the Rope and Twine Company. The cart is from the Co-op.

An early view of Wratting Road showing the very bad state of the road, *c.* 1880. The Local Board could only dump hardcore at intervals to level out the deep ruts made by waggons.

A later view of Wratting Road with the school headmaster's house on the left, *c.* 1910, an early home of the Local History Group. Note the low railway bridge across the road which caught many high vehicles out over the years. Station Road is behind the trees on the right.

Haverhill's famous French-style urinal is rarely seen in photographs, but here in 1925 it is almost the centre piece. The small boy on the right is standing outside Boardman's, the estate agents.

Soldiers passing through Haverhill in 1912, when manoeuvres were being held in the area. George V came through Haverhill at this time, while watching and inspecting his troops.

Haverhill North railway station in 1914. Outside the station was a large open yard which was often deep with mud, so a cobbled and brick path provided a route to the main door in 1890.

Haverhill North station in Edwardian days. The small girl is standing near the W.H. Smith bookstall. The house to the left of the waggon is in Wratting Road.

In 1910 General Booth of the Salvation Army came to Haverhill to give a talk in the town hall. Here he is arriving at Haverhill GER station.

Haverhill's Colne Valley station, also known as Haverhill South, seen in 1957. The white building was put up by Silcock's, a cattle food firm, and the lorries are loading from the Co-op coal yard.

It is 1896 and a group of mainly children are gathered outside the Temperance Hotel, carrying small baskets, possibly for an outing to a local beauty spot.

Haverhill Rope, Twine and Sack Company's shop next to the Rose and Crown Inn, as seen in 1960.

A quiet view in 1916 of the junctions of Queen Street, Wratting Road and Withersfield Road. A third extension has been built on the Rose and Crown, on the left, while the inn sign is precariously placed on the opposite side of the road. The weekly cattle market was held behind the buildings on the left, where the Corn Exchange can be seen, built in 1889, just behind the street lamp. Haverhill's famous fountain or trough is on the right, given to the town in 1904 by Lady Malcolm. It was removed in the 1960s for road reconstruction, and was thought to have been lost, but came back to the town in 1998 to be placed in Queen Street, near Queens Square. Instead of containing water it is now planted with flowers to add some colour to the street. Note the solitary lamppost standing on its own island. On at least one occasion, it was knocked down by a passing vehicle.

Part of the procession for the 1911 Coronation celebrations is waiting to move off from outside the Rose and Crown, with most of the people in their Sunday best.

One of the few photographs known of the weekly livestock market, held behind the new Corn Exchange in Withersfield Road. The site is no longer in operation and is now occupied by a car park.

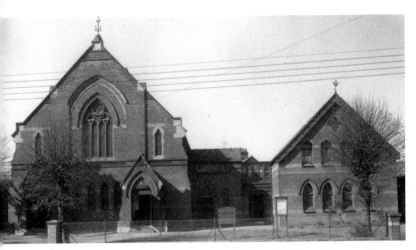

The West End Congregational church and schoolroom built in 1891, pictured here in 1970.

During the training manoenvres in 1912, the army airship Gamma was seen passing over the West End church, in Withersfield Road.

The 1st Haverhill West End church scout troup of 1926.

From the Haverhill & District Sunday School Union Pageant in 1928 comes a photograph of the West End Church group dressed as North American Indians.

The West End Congregational church was selected by the BBC for one of its broadcasts of the popular Sunday Half Hour programmes in 1948, and here the congregation pose for the camera.

Just off Withersfield Road past the school is Broad Street, a small *cul-de-sac* of late Victorian houses, virtually unchanged since the time they were built.

Unveiling & Dedication of HAVERHILL WAR MEMORIAL

With the churchyards of St Mary's and other religious institutions becoming full, the cemetery in Withersfield Road was opened in 1867, complete with a small chapel which served all the denominations of the town, and a caretaker's house. The burial ground was divided, with Church of England graves on the left and Nonconformist ones on the right. It was here in November 1920 that the Haverhill war memorial was dedicated and unveiled by Lt-Gen. Sir Charles Briggs.

Opposite above: It was around the area of the Crowland Road junction with Withersfield Road that the 1958 floods were at their worst. A lone policeman battles through waist high water, a photograph that made the front pages of some national newspapers.

Opposite below: Baldock's Garage, a small garage on the western edge of the town as seen around 1960. It was opened in the 1920s as an addition to the firm of E.W. Baldock, agricultural engineers, which was founded in 1880.

Baldock's steam engines were a regular sight around the Haverhill district. Here in 1912 an engine is pulling a loaded metal wheeled cart outside the railway station.

On the western edge of the town stood Melbourne Bridge garage, quite a big building, now demolished. The road to Withersfield can be seen on the left.

Four

Camps Road to Burton End

From St Mary's church tower the Camps Road area of Haverhill can be seen in 1955. The large building in the middle foreground is the Eastern Counties bus garage, and on its right the garden of Burton Cottage with its small pergola. The coned set of buildings are part of the old Christmas Brewery, now the doctors' surgery, while behind these are the Downs allotments and in the distance the houses in Crowland Road. An interesting building can be recognized towards the top left corner, the unusual shaped hut which housed the first cinema in Haverhill, built in a Chauntry Road garden in 1911, and called the 'Premier Picture Palace'.

Mr Mynott's saddlery shop in Camps Road, situated between the Queen Street corner and the Bull Inn. The saddler was an indispensable member of the community in Edwardian times.

Burton Cottage as it appeared in 1950. Standing outside are the Boardman family.

Above: Burton Cottage looking in a sorry state after a fire which gutted it in 1987. The iron balcony seen on the left now resides in the library built on this spot. The barge board over the front porch was also salvaged, and stored by the local history group.

Right: Probably Haverhill's most interesting character, Barnabas Webb, who lived in the late-eighteenth and early-nineteenth centuries. His diaries are a great insight into the town and its people during his lifetime. He was a weaver by trade, and once lived in the old Burton Cottage.

Above: Tucked away in a small pathway off Camps Road called Upper Downs Slade, and next to the new Christmas Maltings Health Centre, is the Primitive Baptist chapel built in 1828. It stands in a small burial ground, which seems never to have been used as such.

Left: The old maltings of the Christmas Brewery are shown here as the home of Premier Travel coaches, when the buildings were badly damaged in the gales of 1976.

Chauntry Road, Haverhill

Above: Running parallel with Camps Road from the Factory is Chauntry Road, a quiet spot although near to the town centre. This early morning view from 1912, shows the milk cart making its rounds.

Right: A terrace at one side of the Recreation Ground, quaintly named Chainey Pieces seen from Recreation Road.

Nunns Yard, near the Black Horse public house in Camps Road. This is now one of the few yards left when once they were to be found all around the town.

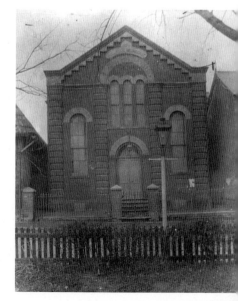

The Methodist chapel, built in 1874. During the first twenty years of its foundation, from 1854 onwards, the congregation held open-air services, and also used an old bakehouse, a room in Leys Yard, and then the old Temperance Hall in Chauntry Road.

The Methodist chapel ladies on Wesley Day, 1938.

The Methodist chapel youngsters always entered into the social life of the town and are seen here winning the Maypole Dancing Competition in 1911.

The Recreation Ground was opened on 24 May 1900, Queen Victoria's birthday, and consisted of twelve acres donated by Mr W.B. Gurteen. A double row of trees, 249 limes and others, were planted around the boundary, making a pleasant walk. A caretaker was first appointed but later it came under the umbrella of the Council. The iron railings which enclosed the 'Rec' were taken away for the war effort in 1940. On the opening day the children soon made use of the seesaw, while to the left is seen a part of Chainey Pieces. Behind the children there is no sign as yet of Recreation Road, since this was built later in 1911.

Opposite above: The bandstand on the Recreation Ground being put to use, with a local band attracting a small audience, on a weekend in 1946.

Opposite below: Another structure on the Recreation Ground was the elaborate shelter built for and called the 'Old Folks Rest'. It was paid for by Conrad Webb and has now been demolished.

Above: Looking down at old Haverhill from Helions Wood in 1874. The large bulk of Gurteen's factory with its high chimney fills the centre, while the track seen on the left is Mill Road. The wide expanse of allotments are now covered by the Helion Park Estate.

Right: Paske's Mill which stood on Mill Hill. There has been a windmill on this spot since the seventeenth century.

Opposite above: At the bottom of the Recreation Ground the stream which ran beside Camps Road down to the town had been left open, giving the area a rural touch. This spot, pictured in 1907, became known as the local lovers' walk.

Opposite below: The 'Rec' has been the scene for many of Haverhill's activities over the years. With the coming of commercial television to the region, the Anglia TV Roadshow came to the Recreation Ground in 1959. The special guests arrived by helicopter, on a sunny day in September.

The bottom of Paske's windmill has survived, now being attached to a modern bungalow. It was used for several purposes including, at one time, a rather unusual garden shed.

Looking down Mill Road towards the town centre. The small sweet shop on the right was a favourite with the local children, but has now disappeared, along with all the houses on the right.

The British Legion Hall was originally called the Drill Hall, the headquarters of the Haverhill Volunteer Regiment. Standing in Burton End opposite the Rose Tavern, it has now been adapted as a private house.

Seen here in 1956, Weavers Row is a block of twelve weavers' cottages. The ground floor contained the living quarters, the middle floor was occupied by the loom, and had a large window at either end, while the top storey was used for bedrooms or stores.

Standing on the edge of the town is the waterworks, built in 1897.

By 1923 a swimming bath had been created at the waterworks, shown here with a group of girls. The water was described as mucky and greenish, and the bottom could not be seen. The sexes were strictly segregated.

Five

Round About

The Pightle was a short street running parallel with Queen Street, and for a while served as the bus station for the town. The passengers were dropped off and collected on the right of the picture, next to the river, which goes on to join the River Stour at Wixoe to the east of Haverhill. On the left are the police station and the courthouse built in 1886, which later moved to Camps Road. The police station was later relocated to Swan Lane, its present home, while the courthouse remained in Camps Road. The original buildings have recently been demolished. The Pightle is now part of the Relief Road, together with Lordscroft Lane seen in the distance.

Above: Taylor's Mill in the Pightle in 1900. The mill was built around 1860. Fred Taylor also built a row of houses next door in 1884, calling them Boyton Terrace, as he lived at Boyton Hall. The Hovis Bread & Flour Co. acquired the business in 1915.

Right: Hovis Mill which took the place of Taylor's Mill in 1936. During the Second World War the new mill was often running twenty-four hours a day to help provide food. The town's air raid siren was placed on the mill roof.

Opposite above: Haverhill's outdoor swimming pool in The Pightle was built by the Haverhill Urban District Council in 1931, but now lies under the police station car park.

Opposite below: This picture of the old fire station comes from 1958. It stood on the corner of Swan Lane and the Pightle, before the present Fire Station was built on the relief road.

Haverhill Volunteer Fire Brigade goes back to at least the beginning of the nineteenth century. Here, in 1906, they parade in their smart uniforms, shining brass helmets, polished brass buttons and whistles on chains. They all have axes tucked into their belts and one man also has a lifeline. Left to right: William Thake (first engineer), H.B. Thake (fireman), J. Knewstubb (superintendent and council surveyor), H.D. Taylor (fireman), John Chapman (fireman), William Brown (second engineer), D.M. Gurteen (lieutenant), Robert Bridge (captain), and R. Farrant (driver).

Opposite above: The offices of the Haverhill Urban District Council were for many years situated in Swan Lane, shown here in 1954. The police station now occupies this site.

Opposite below: Haverhill's cricket ground was located in the Meadows and at one time one was of the most picturesque in the county. This is a line-up from 1893. Left to right, back row: D. Smith, T. Nicholson, D. Gowers, F.W. Gurteen, S. Pole, J. Bedford. On chairs: W.J. Backler, Dr Hargrave, F.G. Smart (captain), P.F. Taylor, F.J. Mason. On grass: D.M. Gurteen (scorer), D. Whiffing.

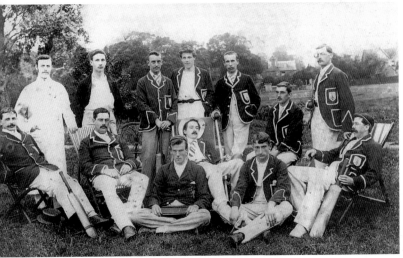

Lordscroft Lane led to the 'Meadows', one of the beauty spots of old Haverhill, with a long double line of trees enclosing the path, now the line of the relief road.

Further along the path, a small wooden footbridge leads off to Meetings Walk; the first house can be seen on the left.

Six

Sport and Leisure

The installation of the Lancashire Boiler in 1925 at D. Gurteen and Sons, Chauntry Mill. They moved to their present site in 1876, after operating in premises behind the present day post office. Workers in the local villages were also used, who worked in their own homes, the factory carrier delivering and collecting the work. For many years they were the largest employers in Haverhill, and in 1888 it was noted they employed 1,500 hands, two thirds of them women, and another 1,500 outworkers. Left to right: F.D. Unwin, F.W. Gurteen, D.M. Gurteen, D.M. Gurteen Jnr, O.G. Smart, A.G. Smart, ? Hills (boiler engineer), C.S. Gurteen, H. Gurteen, T. Farrant, W. Spicer, D. Mizon.

A full line-up of the Haverhill railway staff in 1920, from both stations: the GER (Haverhill North) and the Colne Valley (Haverhill South).

Haverhill Rope, Twine and Sack Co. was established in 1899 with the factory in Burton End. This shows the old 'rope walk', a rather primitive open-fronted structure built of timber and corrugated iron.

The staff outside the new 'Rope Walk', *c.* 1920, now preserved in the Museum of Rural Life at Stowmarket. Left to right: W. Whiting, B. Radford, W. Mayes, B. Whiting, -?-, P. Whiting, G. Sizer, J. Downey, -?-, W. Mayes.

Staff of Mason and Son the builders, photographed in the garden of Mr C. Mason, Sussex House, in the High Street, *c.* 1928. Mason's built many of the important structures in Haverhill. Left to right: back row: Harry Cracknell, ? Whiffing, Fred Whiting, Albert Poole, Stan Wiseman, Jim Newsby. Middle row: Frank Rowlingson, George White, James Sizer, Bob Wiseman, Joe Pannell. Front row: ? Sizer, Peter Meade, ? Darking, Fred Sizer, Hector Robinson.

Haverhill Urban District Council and Bates, Ellison & Co. offices, in 1938. The staff are, left to right: J. Beasley, W. Whitfield, P. Pavey, M. Dilley. At the window is Mr Beasley's daughter Marjorie.

Burton garage home of Burton Coaches, c. 1960. This was a local firm whose original depot was on the corner of Clements Lane and Camps Road. They flourished mainly as private hire specialists and are still going strong today.

Right: Film operator in
the projection room of
the Playhouse cinema
in the High Street, *c.*
1970. The cinema closed
in 1973, after showing
The Boy Friend.

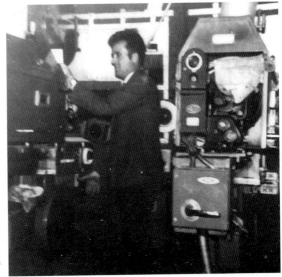

Below: Nunn's Willow
Works on the Sturmer
Road. Stephen Nunn is
standing on the left, and
the man in the centre with
hands on his waist is Mr
Page. This industry has been
closed for many years now.

Towards the end of the 1950s, the 'Town Expansion Scheme' was agreed upon, which meant new factories re-locating in Haverhill. This view, taken from the top of the old Colne Valley railway bridge in Bumpstead Road, shows the new Industrial Estate beginning to take shape. The road leading from the Bumpstead Road is Holland's Road, and the first factory taking shape on the junction is Mansols. The group of cottages behind this factory stand on the corner of the road to Helions Bumpstead. They have now disappeared. On the horizon to the left is Copse Hall Farm.

Seven

The Wind of Change

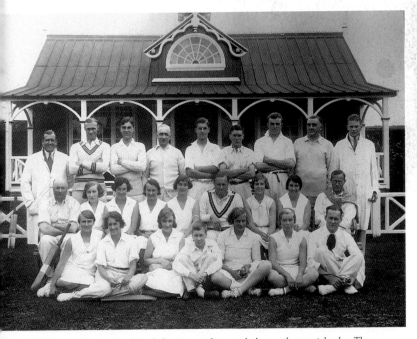

In 1931 the gentleman played the ladies in a cricket match, but under special rules. The gentlemen had to bat and bowl left-handed, and use baseball bats instead of cricket bats. Left to right, back row: W.V. Gurteen, Jim Unwin, -?-, George Unwin, Maynard Gurteen, -?-, Phil Taylor, -?-. Middle row: Dr Sunderland, Peggy Taylor, Wendy Bedford, Grace Gurteen, Di Taylor, F.W. Gurteen, Kathleen Unwin, Nora Bedford, C.S. Gurteen. Front row: Freda Emson, Phyllis Boardman, Joyce Taylor, Sam Taylor, Joan Gurteen, J.T. Boardman.

From the early-nineteenth century Haverhill has had a band. This photograph shows the Haverhill Brass Band in 1884, on parade outside the Old Independent Church Manse, together with their transport.

Coming further up to date, this is the Haverhill Co-operative Silver Band, which was founded in 1920. Here they are in 1933.

Above: This rather unusual band, seen here in 1900, is the Haverhill String Band. This was an all male band that entertained mostly at garden parties and fêtes.

Right: One of the best decorated floats in the Coronation celebrations of 1911 was the Volunteer Fire Brigade's entry, featuring a beautifully made cottage with a thatched roof, all pulled by proper horse power. The procession is lining up outside the vicarage, now Anne of Cleves House, part of which is visible on the right.

Coronation Day in 1902 shows members of the Church Lad's Brigade and the Old Independent Boy's Life Brigade standing to attention while the Volunteers fire a salute on the Hamlet Croft.

Haverhill's Gala always brought out some ambitious floats: this was the Co-op's contribution in 1956.

There have been many football clubs in the town over the years. This is Haverhill St Mary's FC from the 1920/21 season.

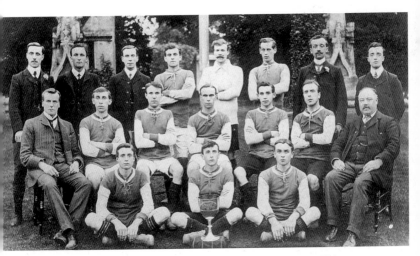

Another church club was the Old Independent Institute FC, seen here in 1914.

Haverhill West End Institute's Football Club line up in 1921/22.

BRITISH LEGION BAND HAVERHILL
(The March Past).

The march past at the British Legion Rally in Haverhill, around 1925.

Haverhill Quoits Club, c. 1900. Their headquarters were at the Red Lion in the High Street, and they played in the yard behind the inn.

Nothing very much is known about the group of men, young and old, who willingly posed for this photograph. The occasion was the Teetotallers Exhibition in Haverhill at around the turn of the century.

Left: Easter Monday, 4 April 1908, brought enough snow to enable this fine snowman to be made in one of the town's gardens.

Below: All the religious denominations had their Sunday school treat for the children. This is the Salvation Army setting out for an exciting afternoon in 1916.

Opposite above: A group of Haverhill's young ladies before setting out on the town's first 'Flag Day' in 1916.

Opposite below: Mrs Fell of the Rose & Crown was always looked upon as one of the best caterers in the town, and she is seen here, on the left, setting up for a party. The location is thought to be Sturmer Hall and the date, around 1900. Note the tea urn and the crockery basket.

Easter Mon: 20.4.08.

The Haverhill Dramatic Players production of *Blithe Spirit*, c. 1950.

The Bull Inn Cork Club of 1905.

Fancy dress entrants at the West End church fête in Mason's garden in 1952.

A group of ladies with their bonny babies pictured in the grandstand at the Hamlet Croft. It is possibly one of the galas of the late 1940s.

In 1956, the famous
Battle of Britain pilot,
Douglas Bader, paid a
visit to the Haverhill
Air Training Corp.
Here he is inspecting
them in Mount Road.

Douglas Bader also found time to
have an informal chat with some of
the cadets at their headquarters.

The Haverhill Scouts were awarded the 3rd prize at the George V Coronation Celebrations in 1911.

A group of Gurteen's long-serving employees (over fifty years) in 1920. Left to right, back row: W. Rowlingson, Miss E. Basham, James Sizer, Mrs E. Coates, David Scott, William Poole, Walter Page, Mrs E. Humphrey. Middle row: Harry Whiting, Miss J. Free, Jonas Whiting, Miss F. Skilton, Frank Backler, Mrs S. Thake, William Wash, Mrs E. Poole. Front row: Alfred Burton, Miss E. Rowlingson, Walter Rash, Jabez Gurteen, Miss S. Farrant, Walter Basham, Mrs E. Jobson.

Right: A Haverhill ex-servicemen's dinner in the town hall in the 1970s.

Below: St John's Ambulance Brigade on parade on the Recreation Ground in 1957.

Eight

The Wind of Change

The early 1960s saw Haverhill as the 'Pioneers of Town Expansion'; this meant more shops in the High Street and Queen Street. The variously-shaped small family shops were the first to go, to make way for new buildings, a fact mourned by many of the native townsfolk. Here we see the old making way for the new in Queen Street. The small shop that was next to be demolished was Baldry's radio and television shop, to be followed by Hayward's Garage. The new shop on the right now forms part of the new Queens Square.

Left: By 1957, there was a developing traffic problem, with the main road going through the centre of the town. A view from the top floor of the Co-operative building shows how the narrow Queen Street struggled to deal with the problem.

Below: Construction of the new inner relief road was started by Al. R.C. Poole, on a tractor, in 1953. This new road followed the route of the Meadows footpath, from Hamlet Green to Lordscroft Lane.

New estates were needed to house the newcomers. This is part of the first one, the Clements. Three young children sit and view their new surroundings.

The youngsters soon found enough space to play on the Clements estate, which won an award for its designer.

More families meant more schools were needed. The Castle Manor School in Eastern Avenue on the Parkway estate, was opened in May 1960, taking the place of the Victorian Cangle School, formerly the local Board School, in Withersfield Road. Extensions were added later, to the right-hand side of the original building.

Opposite above: New estates meant more shops. This parade of shops is on the Parkway Extension estate.

Opposite below: One of the new shopping malls in the High Street was Jubilee Walk, linking the coach station with the High Street.

Looking from the Clements estate across the town. The new houses on the far right of the hill are part of the Chalkstone estate, while the trees in the centre of the photograph surround the recreation ground.

Haverhill Urban District Council in their brand new Council Offices in Queen Street. They are, left to right, back row: William Elkins, Norman Pryke, Reg Poole, Horace Eves, William Blake (clerk to the council) Bernard Simms (chairman of the HUDC) Bob Basham, Mr Foster, John Rowlinson, Vera Godden. In front are the officers. Left to right: Patrick Hewitt (housing manager) Reginald Bank (public health inspector) John Johnson (engineer and surveyor), Frederick Altorfer (treasurer). This was in the 1960s before the St Edmundsbury became the ruling body in Haverhill.